HOUSEHOLD BUDGET PLANNER

Copyright 2015

Month__________

INCOME
RENT
GAS
GROCERIES
LEFT FOR BILLS

EXPENSE	DUE	AMOUNT	PAID	BALANCE LEFT

Month__________

INCOME
RENT
GAS
GROCERIES
LEFT FOR BILLS

EXPENSE	DUE	AMOUNT	PAID	BALANCE LEFT

Month__________

INCOME
RENT
GAS
GROCERIES
LEFT FOR BILLS

EXPENSE	DUE	AMOUNT	PAID	BALANCE LEFT

Month__________

INCOME
RENT
GAS
GROCERIES
LEFT FOR BILLS

EXPENSE	DUE	AMOUNT	PAID	BALANCE LEFT

Month_________

INCOME
RENT
GAS
GROCERIES
LEFT FOR BILLS

EXPENSE	DUE	AMOUNT	PAID	BALANCE LEFT

Month__________

INCOME
RENT
GAS
GROCERIES
LEFT FOR BILLS

EXPENSE	DUE	AMOUNT	PAID	BALANCE LEFT

Month__________

INCOME
RENT
GAS
GROCERIES
LEFT FOR BILLS

EXPENSE	DUE	AMOUNT	PAID	BALANCE LEFT

Month__________

INCOME
RENT
GAS
GROCERIES
LEFT FOR BILLS

EXPENSE	DUE	AMOUNT	PAID	BALANCE LEFT

Month_________

INCOME
RENT
GAS
GROCERIES
LEFT FOR BILLS

EXPENSE	DUE	AMOUNT	PAID	BALANCE LEFT

EXPENSE	DUE	AMOUNT	PAID	BALANCE LEFT

Month__________

INCOME
RENT
GAS
GROCERIES
LEFT FOR BILLS

EXPENSE	DUE	AMOUNT	PAID	BALANCE LEFT

Month___________

INCOME
RENT
GAS
GROCERIES
LEFT FOR BILLS

EXPENSE	DUE	AMOUNT	PAID	BALANCE LEFT

Month_________

INCOME
RENT
GAS
GROCERIES
LEFT FOR BILLS

EXPENSE	DUE	AMOUNT	PAID	BALANCE LEFT

Month__________

INCOME
RENT
GAS
GROCERIES
LEFT FOR BILLS

EXPENSE	DUE	AMOUNT	PAID	BALANCE LEFT

Month_________

INCOME
RENT
GAS
GROCERIES
LEFT FOR BILLS

EXPENSE	DUE	AMOUNT	PAID	BALANCE LEFT

Month__________

INCOME
RENT
GAS
GROCERIES
LEFT FOR BILLS

EXPENSE	DUE	AMOUNT	PAID	BALANCE LEFT

Month__________

INCOME
RENT
GAS
GROCERIES
LEFT FOR BILLS

EXPENSE	DUE	AMOUNT	PAID	BALANCE LEFT

Month__________

INCOME
RENT
GAS
GROCERIES
LEFT FOR BILLS

EXPENSE	DUE	AMOUNT	PAID	BALANCE LEFT

Month__________

INCOME
RENT
GAS
GROCERIES
LEFT FOR BILLS

EXPENSE	DUE	AMOUNT	PAID	BALANCE LEFT

Month__________

INCOME
RENT
GAS
GROCERIES
LEFT FOR BILLS

EXPENSE	DUE	AMOUNT	PAID	BALANCE LEFT

INCOME
RENT
GAS
GROCERIES
LEFT FOR BILLS

EXPENSE	DUE	AMOUNT	PAID	BALANCE LEFT

Month__________

INCOME
RENT
GAS
GROCERIES
LEFT FOR BILLS

EXPENSE	DUE	AMOUNT	PAID	BALANCE LEFT

Month_________

INCOME
RENT
GAS
GROCERIES
LEFT FOR BILLS

EXPENSE	DUE	AMOUNT	PAID	BALANCE LEFT

Month__________

INCOME
RENT
GAS
GROCERIES
LEFT FOR BILLS

EXPENSE	DUE	AMOUNT	PAID	BALANCE LEFT

Month__________

INCOME
RENT
GAS
GROCERIES
LEFT FOR BILLS

EXPENSE	DUE	AMOUNT	PAID	BALANCE LEFT

Month__________

INCOME
RENT
GAS
GROCERIES
LEFT FOR BILLS

EXPENSE	DUE	AMOUNT	PAID	BALANCE LEFT

Month__________

INCOME
RENT
GAS
GROCERIES
LEFT FOR BILLS

EXPENSE	DUE	AMOUNT	PAID	BALANCE LEFT

Month__________

INCOME
RENT
GAS
GROCERIES
LEFT FOR BILLS

EXPENSE	DUE	AMOUNT	PAID	BALANCE LEFT

Month__________

INCOME
RENT
GAS
GROCERIES
LEFT FOR BILLS

EXPENSE	DUE	AMOUNT	PAID	BALANCE LEFT

Month_________

INCOME
RENT
GAS
GROCERIES
LEFT FOR BILLS

EXPENSE	DUE	AMOUNT	PAID	BALANCE LEFT

Month__________

INCOME
RENT
GAS
GROCERIES
LEFT FOR BILLS

EXPENSE	DUE	AMOUNT	PAID	BALANCE LEFT

Month__________

INCOME
RENT
GAS
GROCERIES
LEFT FOR BILLS

EXPENSE	DUE	AMOUNT	PAID	BALANCE LEFT

Month__________

INCOME
RENT
GAS
GROCERIES
LEFT FOR BILLS

EXPENSE	DUE	AMOUNT	PAID	BALANCE LEFT

Month__________

INCOME
RENT
GAS
GROCERIES
LEFT FOR BILLS

EXPENSE	DUE	AMOUNT	PAID	BALANCE LEFT

Month__________

INCOME
RENT
GAS
GROCERIES
LEFT FOR BILLS

EXPENSE	DUE	AMOUNT	PAID	BALANCE LEFT

Month__________

INCOME
RENT
GAS
GROCERIES
LEFT FOR BILLS

EXPENSE	DUE	AMOUNT	PAID	BALANCE LEFT

Month__________

INCOME
RENT
GAS
GROCERIES
LEFT FOR BILLS

EXPENSE	DUE	AMOUNT	PAID	BALANCE LEFT

Month__________

INCOME
RENT
GAS
GROCERIES
LEFT FOR BILLS

EXPENSE	DUE	AMOUNT	PAID	BALANCE LEFT

Month__________

INCOME
RENT
GAS
GROCERIES
LEFT FOR BILLS

EXPENSE	DUE	AMOUNT	PAID	BALANCE LEFT

Month_________

INCOME
RENT
GAS
GROCERIES
LEFT FOR BILLS

EXPENSE	DUE	AMOUNT	PAID	BALANCE LEFT

Month__________

INCOME
RENT
GAS
GROCERIES
LEFT FOR BILLS

EXPENSE	DUE	AMOUNT	PAID	BALANCE LEFT

Month__________

INCOME
RENT
GAS
GROCERIES
LEFT FOR BILLS

EXPENSE	DUE	AMOUNT	PAID	BALANCE LEFT

Month__________

INCOME
RENT
GAS
GROCERIES
LEFT FOR BILLS

EXPENSE	DUE	AMOUNT	PAID	BALANCE LEFT

Month__________

INCOME
RENT
GAS
GROCERIES
LEFT FOR BILLS

EXPENSE	DUE	AMOUNT	PAID	BALANCE LEFT

Month_________

INCOME
RENT
GAS
GROCERIES
LEFT FOR BILLS

EXPENSE	DUE	AMOUNT	PAID	BALANCE LEFT

Month_________

INCOME
RENT
GAS
GROCERIES
LEFT FOR BILLS

EXPENSE	DUE	AMOUNT	PAID	BALANCE LEFT

Month__________

INCOME
RENT
GAS
GROCERIES
LEFT FOR BILLS

EXPENSE	DUE	AMOUNT	PAID	BALANCE LEFT

Month___________

INCOME
RENT
GAS
GROCERIES
LEFT FOR BILLS

EXPENSE	DUE	AMOUNT	PAID	BALANCE LEFT

Month__________

INCOME
RENT
GAS
GROCERIES
LEFT FOR BILLS

EXPENSE	DUE	AMOUNT	PAID	BALANCE LEFT

Month__________

INCOME
RENT
GAS
GROCERIES
LEFT FOR BILLS

EXPENSE	DUE	AMOUNT	PAID	BALANCE LEFT

Month__________

INCOME
RENT
GAS
GROCERIES
LEFT FOR BILLS

EXPENSE	DUE	AMOUNT	PAID	BALANCE LEFT

Month__________

INCOME
RENT
GAS
GROCERIES
LEFT FOR BILLS

EXPENSE	DUE	AMOUNT	PAID	BALANCE LEFT

Month__________

INCOME
RENT
GAS
GROCERIES
LEFT FOR BILLS

EXPENSE	DUE	AMOUNT	PAID	BALANCE LEFT

Month__________

INCOME
RENT
GAS
GROCERIES
LEFT FOR BILLS

EXPENSE	DUE	AMOUNT	PAID	BALANCE LEFT

Month__________

INCOME
RENT
GAS
GROCERIES
LEFT FOR BILLS

EXPENSE	DUE	AMOUNT	PAID	BALANCE LEFT

Month__________

INCOME
RENT
GAS
GROCERIES
LEFT FOR BILLS

EXPENSE	DUE	AMOUNT	PAID	BALANCE LEFT

Month__________

INCOME
RENT
GAS
GROCERIES
LEFT FOR BILLS

EXPENSE	DUE	AMOUNT	PAID	BALANCE LEFT

Month__________

INCOME
RENT
GAS
GROCERIES
LEFT FOR BILLS

EXPENSE	DUE	AMOUNT	PAID	BALANCE LEFT

Month__________

INCOME
RENT
GAS
GROCERIES
LEFT FOR BILLS

EXPENSE	DUE	AMOUNT	PAID	BALANCE LEFT

Month__________

INCOME
RENT
GAS
GROCERIES
LEFT FOR BILLS

EXPENSE	DUE	AMOUNT	PAID	BALANCE LEFT

Month_________

INCOME
RENT
GAS
GROCERIES
LEFT FOR BILLS

EXPENSE	DUE	AMOUNT	PAID	BALANCE LEFT

Month__________

INCOME
RENT
GAS
GROCERIES
LEFT FOR BILLS

EXPENSE	DUE	AMOUNT	PAID	BALANCE LEFT

Month__________

INCOME
RENT
GAS
GROCERIES
LEFT FOR BILLS

EXPENSE	DUE	AMOUNT	PAID	BALANCE LEFT

Month__________

EXPENSE	DUE	AMOUNT	PAID	BALANCE LEFT

Month_________

INCOME
RENT
GAS
GROCERIES
LEFT FOR BILLS

EXPENSE	DUE	AMOUNT	PAID	BALANCE LEFT

Month________

INCOME
RENT
GAS
GROCERIES
LEFT FOR BILLS

EXPENSE	DUE	AMOUNT	PAID	BALANCE LEFT

Month__________

INCOME
RENT
GAS
GROCERIES
LEFT FOR BILLS

EXPENSE	DUE	AMOUNT	PAID	BALANCE LEFT

Month__________

INCOME
RENT
GAS
GROCERIES
LEFT FOR BILLS

EXPENSE	DUE	AMOUNT	PAID	BALANCE LEFT

INCOME
RENT
GAS
GROCERIES
LEFT FOR BILLS

EXPENSE	DUE	AMOUNT	PAID	BALANCE LEFT

Month_________

INCOME
RENT
GAS
GROCERIES
LEFT FOR BILLS

EXPENSE	DUE	AMOUNT	PAID	BALANCE LEFT

Month_________

INCOME
RENT
GAS
GROCERIES
LEFT FOR BILLS

EXPENSE	DUE	AMOUNT	PAID	BALANCE LEFT

Month___________

INCOME
RENT
GAS
GROCERIES
LEFT FOR BILLS

EXPENSE	DUE	AMOUNT	PAID	BALANCE LEFT

Month__________

INCOME
RENT
GAS
GROCERIES
LEFT FOR BILLS

EXPENSE	DUE	AMOUNT	PAID	BALANCE LEFT

Month__________

INCOME
RENT
GAS
GROCERIES
LEFT FOR BILLS

EXPENSE	DUE	AMOUNT	PAID	BALANCE LEFT

Month__________

INCOME
RENT
GAS
GROCERIES
LEFT FOR BILLS

EXPENSE	DUE	AMOUNT	PAID	BALANCE LEFT

Month__________

INCOME
RENT
GAS
GROCERIES
LEFT FOR BILLS

EXPENSE	DUE	AMOUNT	PAID	BALANCE LEFT

EXPENSE	DUE	AMOUNT	PAID	BALANCE LEFT

Month__________

INCOME
RENT
GAS
GROCERIES
LEFT FOR BILLS

EXPENSE	DUE	AMOUNT	PAID	BALANCE LEFT

INCOME
RENT
GAS
GROCERIES
LEFT FOR BILLS

EXPENSE	DUE	AMOUNT	PAID	BALANCE LEFT

Month________

INCOME
RENT
GAS
GROCERIES
LEFT FOR BILLS

EXPENSE	DUE	AMOUNT	PAID	BALANCE LEFT

EXPENSE	DUE	AMOUNT	PAID	BALANCE LEFT

Month__________

INCOME
RENT
GAS
GROCERIES
LEFT FOR BILLS

EXPENSE	DUE	AMOUNT	PAID	BALANCE LEFT

Month__________

INCOME
RENT
GAS
GROCERIES
LEFT FOR BILLS

EXPENSE	DUE	AMOUNT	PAID	BALANCE LEFT

Month__________

INCOME
RENT
GAS
GROCERIES
LEFT FOR BILLS

EXPENSE	DUE	AMOUNT	PAID	BALANCE LEFT

Month_________

Bills

INCOME
RENT
GAS
GROCERIES
LEFT FOR BILLS

EXPENSE	DUE	AMOUNT	PAID	BALANCE LEFT

Month__________

INCOME
RENT
GAS
GROCERIES
LEFT FOR BILLS

EXPENSE	DUE	AMOUNT	PAID	BALANCE LEFT

Month__________

INCOME
RENT
GAS
GROCERIES
LEFT FOR BILLS

EXPENSE	DUE	AMOUNT	PAID	BALANCE LEFT

Month__________

INCOME
RENT
GAS
GROCERIES
LEFT FOR BILLS

EXPENSE	DUE	AMOUNT	PAID	BALANCE LEFT

Month__________

INCOME
RENT
GAS
GROCERIES
LEFT FOR BILLS

EXPENSE	DUE	AMOUNT	PAID	BALANCE LEFT

Month__________

INCOME
RENT
GAS
GROCERIES
LEFT FOR BILLS

EXPENSE	DUE	AMOUNT	PAID	BALANCE LEFT

Month__________

INCOME
RENT
GAS
GROCERIES
LEFT FOR BILLS

EXPENSE	DUE	AMOUNT	PAID	BALANCE LEFT

Month__________

INCOME
RENT
GAS
GROCERIES
LEFT FOR BILLS

EXPENSE	DUE	AMOUNT	PAID	BALANCE LEFT

Month_________

INCOME
RENT
GAS
GROCERIES
LEFT FOR BILLS

EXPENSE	DUE	AMOUNT	PAID	BALANCE LEFT

Month_________

INCOME
RENT
GAS
GROCERIES
LEFT FOR BILLS

EXPENSE	DUE	AMOUNT	PAID	BALANCE LEFT

Month__________

INCOME
RENT
GAS
GROCERIES
LEFT FOR BILLS

EXPENSE	DUE	AMOUNT	PAID	BALANCE LEFT

Month__________

INCOME
RENT
GAS
GROCERIES
LEFT FOR BILLS

EXPENSE	DUE	AMOUNT	PAID	BALANCE LEFT

Month__________

INCOME
RENT
GAS
GROCERIES
LEFT FOR BILLS

EXPENSE	DUE	AMOUNT	PAID	BALANCE LEFT

Month________

INCOME
RENT
GAS
GROCERIES
LEFT FOR BILLS

EXPENSE	DUE	AMOUNT	PAID	BALANCE LEFT

Month__________

INCOME
RENT
GAS
GROCERIES
LEFT FOR BILLS

EXPENSE	DUE	AMOUNT	PAID	BALANCE LEFT

Month_____________

INCOME
RENT
GAS
GROCERIES
LEFT FOR BILLS

EXPENSE	DUE	AMOUNT	PAID	BALANCE LEFT

Month__________

INCOME
RENT
GAS
GROCERIES
LEFT FOR BILLS

EXPENSE	DUE	AMOUNT	PAID	BALANCE LEFT

Month__________

INCOME
RENT
GAS
GROCERIES
LEFT FOR BILLS

EXPENSE	DUE	AMOUNT	PAID	BALANCE LEFT

Month__________

INCOME
RENT
GAS
GROCERIES
LEFT FOR BILLS

EXPENSE	DUE	AMOUNT	PAID	BALANCE LEFT

Month__________

INCOME
RENT
GAS
GROCERIES
LEFT FOR BILLS

EXPENSE	DUE	AMOUNT	PAID	BALANCE LEFT